www.finishinglinepress.com

Retracing My Steps

New Women's Voices Series, No. 144

poems by

Jayne Moore Waldrop

Finishing Line Press
Georgetown, Kentucky

Retracing My Steps

New Women's Voices Series, No. 144

For my parents

ACKNOWLEDGMENTS

The epigraph is a brief quote from p. 209 from *All About Love* by bell
hooks. Copyright © 2000 by Gloria Watkins. Reprinted by permission of
HarperCollins Publishers.

"The Other Side" was written in response to Kentucky Poet Laureate George
Ella Lyon's poem "Where I'm From." For more information about the poem
or the I Am From Project, see http://www.georgeellalyon.com/where.html.

"Expat Elegy," "Retracing My Steps" and "Drowned Town" originally
appeared in the *2018 Anthology of Appalachian Writers* published by
Shepherd University.

"Drowned Town" was selected as a poetry winner in *Kentucky Monthly
Magazine's* 2018 Literary Contest.

"Coming through Cumberland Gap" originally appeared in *The Paddock
Review*.

"The Row" originally appeared in *The Heartland Review*

Publisher: Leah Maines
Editor: Christen Kincaid
Cover Art and Design: John Lackey
Author Photo: Tim Webb

Printed in the USA on acid-free paper.
Order online: www.finishinglinepress.com
also available on amazon.com

Author inquiries and mail orders:
Finishing Line Press
P. O. Box 1626
Georgetown, Kentucky 40324
U. S. A.

Table of Contents

Mindful remembering lets us put the broken bits and pieces of our hearts together again.

—bell hooks, *All About Love*

Retracing My Steps

Blurred by inattention, life
passes unobserved and I
must remind myself where I
am. I no longer notice
details along the way to
the office, the grocery,
the bathroom, the bed, but when
I set out to retrace a
lonely, forgotten footpath,
kicking up dust, leaves, debris,
I conjure a younger self.
She finds my hand, guides, nudges,
forces me to remember
her and who we used to be.

Coming through Cumberland Gap

The well-marked trail leads straight uphill,
crossing a stream that roars and echoes
through a cave, once a shelter for travelers.
The water cuts through generations of stone,
nine generations to be exact since my people
walked this way. My thighs and lungs strain
but I push on, shod in appropriate footwear,
swathed in tick repellant, lathered in sunscreen,
energized by abundant color and surprise along
the path. Shocking pink blossoms line redbud
branches to frame electric blue skies,
and patches of wildflowers vary with shade
or sun through the woods. How hard, I think
as I climb, it must have been to head off
into the wilderness, to find the notch between
mountains for admission to a place called
Kentucky. The path wasn't new and it wasn't
theirs, but one long worn by others before
we claimed it and made it our own. While I
can't change the history of loss and taking,
the road conjures those who came before. My
eight-great-grandmother came on foot
with children who were surely hungry, tired,
and with soiled pants. Was it her idea to make
the journey? Did she believe it was her way
to a better life? Were they cold, barefoot, sick,
scared, snakebit, peaked? Her risky story makes
me feel modern, fragile, and in awe
of what it took to make it through the gap.

Pleiades

The sisters, born years apart,
by choice strewn lightyears distant,
greet one another with an
embrace on most holidays,
a birthday card in the mail,
a chill when life hammers yet
another wedge between them.
Sometimes it has been the loves
in their lives that divide them.
Sometimes it has been the race
to come in first, to be best,
smartest, sweetest, prettiest,
best, most perfect, most beloved,
best girl of the bunch. In their
collective unconscious they
sense fierce, relentless ranking
going on, a need to win,
to beat the competition
both at home and in the world
as if some never-final
leaderboard keeps scores for each
one. There comes a time, with age
or love or accumulated
sense of self, when they long for
reunion as sisters. They
break away from rivalry
to find a path beyond the
breach, to reach out, grasping for
the powerful, nourishing
cord that strengthens each one and
joins them together for life.

Expat Elegy

Expatriate:
'A person who lives outside their native country' (Oxford)
'Living in a foreign land' (Merriam-Webster's)

They were Appalachian expats,
transplanted hillbillies but best not
call them that unless you, too, are
from the mountains. Unlike the
Clampetts, they didn't strike oil
or gas or mine an unknown seam,
nor did they head to Beverly Hills.
They loaded up and left home for
a multitude of reasons, survival
being high on the list. They were
refugees from another war on coal,
I reckon, long before Barack Hussein
Obama was ever born, wherever that
was, and before the EPA ever existed.
During another downturn in coal
country, they ran a store and made
the noble mistake of extending credit
for food as they witnessed neighbors
go hungry, knowing full well that
desperate people without jobs rarely
repay debts. Left holding an empty
bag, broke and nearly broken,
their only way out was…out.

Traveling westward toward a setting sun,
they resettled in a place flat and fertile,
a boom town known as Atomic City.
Not a mountain in sight, not a rock in
the soil, the landscape was as foreign
as the moon with a sky way too wide.
They were Appalachian expats, exiled
to a new country, displaced to a different
culture. They found work, missed home

and Mommy as their ears adjusted
to a twang as flat as the land.

They spent long hours in town,
daylight to dark, selling cars,
keeping books, pleasing the boss,
building an American dream
for the next generation. They saved,
did without, bought an old house with
enough ground for a garden and a barn,
their form of insurance against hunger.

At a time when the world pushed
to be midcentury modern, the expats
stayed true to themselves and the old
ways. They planted by the signs,
canned kraut, dried apples, strung
beans for winter, and pulled out
the belt when they needed to. They
drank cooled coffee from saucers
and slept under a stack of homemade
quilts that varied in depth with the
season. They kept their people close
and the mountains alive with
stories of acorn-eating hogs,
churchhouse shouts, decorated
graves, and a framed photo
spread from *Life* magazine
of the big and busy playground
at their old Dorton School.

Most newcomers to Atomic City
came with engineering degrees
and Midwestern accents. They didn't
know where yonder was, and they
didn't eat their dinner at midday

or their supper of an evening. They couldn't understand why the Appalachian expats would give up hard-earned vacation days, year after year, to spend time not on a beach but up some holler reconnecting with a bunch of hillbillies. They didn't realize that the dream of going home never dies.

The Slip

She wondered if the mare had felt her
foal begin to slip as her body opened
to reject it. Old wives and young vets agree
nothing much can stanch an unsealing
womb. The horse alone knew when
and where, only a bloody smear along
her tail signaled the fatal fetal imperfection.
Wonder if she heard it hit the ground?
Had Nature counted chromosomes then
chosen to pull the plug? If risk of failure
goes up with age, who decides if a
dream is worth the price or the pain?

No doubt she could have done things
differently. Eaten more, eaten less,
rested more, stressed less. Surely
something, someone should be blamed.
But she had been so careful. No
drugs, no alcohol, no cigarettes.
She had examined all the labels,
read all the best birthing books.
She hadn't traveled, over-exerted,
stretched her hands above her head.
She'd had no physical injury or trauma,
at least not since the last dream lost.

Which started with hard cramping. A
trace of red that grew. A splash, the sound
of something small but full, heavy for
its size, slipping into dirty toilet water.
She couldn't bear to look or retrieve
or even call out for help. Feeling faint,
alone, inexplicably shamed by what she
saw, she closed her eyes and flushed.

The vet had called it a *slip*, making it all
seem fluid and effortless, implying a minor
or careless mistake, a misstep, an otherwise
temporary loss of balance. But face-to-face
with the mare, breathing in the barn's layered
scents, she wondered how she'd suffered,
if her belly had knotted in pain, if her blood
had flowed freely, if she wanted to run away.

The Wall: Haiku from A Gated Community

There's an old saying
that fences make good neighbors.
What about brick walls?

A sign greets: Welcome.
Deed Restricted Neighborhood.
No Soliciting.

In other words, STOP.
Don't pass go. We don't want you.
You're not one of us.

All shall abide by
HOA rules as set forth.
No exceptions, please.

No gardens, clotheslines,
livestock, or anything deemed
undesirable.

Approved trees shall be
planted ten feet from the street.
No exceptions, please.

Is neighborliness
permitted within or without
the walls? Check the rules.

The gates close at dusk,
reopen at dawn to let
the hired help back in.

Cameras, burglar
alarms, driveway gates and guns
shall be permitted.

Is the ten-foot fence
not enough to protect you
from those outsiders?

Inside, they accept
that walls keep them safe but block
their view of the world.

"It's a tradeoff," the
HOA president advises,
"one you won't regret."

A few still yearn to
gaze beyond, to see sunrise
or vibrant sunset.

Cul de sacs become
secure deserted islands
in seas of asphalt.

Safe but lonely as
a castaway, one girl dreams
of scaling the wall.

Pie Plate

Of all the things that were hers,
this conjures her spirit more
clearly than the rest, as if
part of her flowed into its
Corning Glass in the high heat
of her Kenmore oven. Plain,
functional, a hint of scallop
along the rim, a tool for a
life spent feeding and serving
us, her way of loving us.
She was part short-order cook,
part food-processing plant, always
moving, rushing, preparing:
the next meal to be served,
half-runners to can, berries
to pick, corn to freeze,
not to mention spelling
words to give out and clothes to
hang on the line. She never
looked for an easy way out.
No ready-made crusts or canned
cherry fillings or box cake
mixes for her, no sir. She
was a made-from-scratch
woman, a farm-to-table
cook before that was a thing,
no matter how long it took
or what it required of her.

When I was little, I begged
for Birds Eye frozen TV
dinners that looked delicious
and nutritious in commercials
with smiling, picture-perfect
families. I wanted that,

to be like everyone else,
to look like everyone else,
to live the processed American dream
where we would all eat the same
store-bought food and live in
identical ranch houses
in subdivisions with themed
street names. I wanted her
to change, to be like other
moms and not have dirt
under her nails when she came
to my school. I wanted her
skin to darken in the sun
scented with Coppertone oil,
lounging beside a pool, not
smelling like sweat in a field
of tomatoes. I wanted
her to take the easy way
out. She never did.

For this year's Thanksgiving meal,
my assignment is pies, enough
to feed thirty. I missed
the bakery's deadline for
ordering, then forgot to
buy crusts at the store. I won't
be taking the easy way out.
I unfold the handwritten
recipe for custard pie
—her writing was her only
fancy thing—then hunt for the
pie plate buried deep inside
a cupboard, remembering
holiday dessert tables

laden with her tasty gifts, still
wondering how she did it all.
I crave uneven piecrusts
imperfectly scored with fork
tines, an occasional weepy
meringue topping or lumpy
cream filling, all signs of love
from a woman offering
everything she had to give.

Eclipse

Last night we retraced our steps
in the moonlight over old
and uneven brick sidewalks.
First time we traveled the route
on a clear summer day, we carried
fresh, bold promises volleyed
before those gathered together
on mahogany pews. The sun shone
on us through stained glass,
tinting our world pink
like bridesmaids dresses and
lilies tied with ribbons.
We strolled, fingers laced,
in anticipation of everything to come.
Our steps matched the rhythm
of pealing bells, our path scouted
by those who loved us—
parents, brothers, sisters,
flowergirls, aunts in gold sequins,
uncles in wide earthtone ties,
and a gaggle of new lawyers
still thirsting for champagne
three days after the exam.
We strode into the future,
fingers entwined,
in search of everything to come.
Some joined us as we walked,
and others left us along the way.
We kept going,
sometimes rushing, pulsing,
or stumbling and tired,
stomping in anger and hurt,
hobbled by sickness and loss.
At times our promises
eclipsed our dreams.

Last night we retraced our steps
in the moonlight,
over worn brick sidewalks
in need of repair but still in service.
Beyond the quieted tower and darkened
windows we found the place
where we once toasted and laughed
and smiled for the cameras.
This time we took our own photograph,
the two of us,
then strolled on, fingers interlocked,
in wonder of everything to come.

The Row

In the heat of the day he's out
there, hoeing, saying weeds
die faster in the hot sun, looking
like he might, too, his shirt
soaked in sweat and covered in dust
stirred by strokes of his hoe. "You
get used to the heat once you're out
here," he says. He keeps a gallon jug
of water in the shade of the pear tree
where he stops to take a drink
as he makes each turn at the far end
of the garden. With a sharpened blade
he cuts into the earth, leveling weeds
and cultivating soil around stalks
of corn, hills of squash, or lines of
beans climbing toward the light, row
after row, season after season, year
upon year. Those who pull into
the long gravel driveway come to
claim a mess of vegetables, unaware
of the labor heaped into every bushel
basket carried off his place. It's
hard work to give freely, to provide
generously, to keep a family fed,
to keep a family together, to love even
when it's undeserved. He never shies
from the hardest, longest row.
Somehow he handles the heat of the day.

Drowned Town

When the lake level is low in winter,
when wind stings and keeps
tourists away, ghosts rise
from the mud and silt left behind
the retreating water. There used to be
a town here. It's easy to forget the old
river town that had survived floods
and soldiers and hard times
but disappeared without defense
when the giant lake rose. The Cumberland
had crept in many times when
too much rain or snow made it swell
beyond its banks but it always slipped back
into its cut-rock channel. The last time
the river stayed, unable to retreat when the
final yards of concrete were poured at the dam,
forever altering nature, sealing fate,
filling streets and houses and emptied
graveyards, already moved to higher ground.
Townspeople had time to get out of the way
but the place could not escape its drowning.
No rescue or resuscitation could save it.

Each year along the shoreline at winter pool
the railroad returns, its rusty spikes
still scattered in mud and sand as if
workers might return any time now
to finish their repairs. Outlines of stone
foundations re-emerge in the shallows,
awaiting carpenters to rebuild walls
and people to come home. Empty,
watery graves remain open, a reminder
of all that was taken. There used to be
a town here. It's easy to forget.

Second Coming

The second baby
is coming soon,
I hope.
I fear,
just as frightened
as first time around.
You'd think I'd relax,
knowing how this works,
but I remember
the pain,
the fear of the unknown,
the losses in between,
but I keep growing,
driven by the possibilities
of love and miracle
most natural, most human yet divine.
Hit me with the drugs, white coat,
and leave me to dig my way to that
place beneath the porch to have this pup.

What Am I to Do Now?

The question runs on a loop
throughout the day, then
speeds up and increases
in volume during
sundowner hours.
No answer satisfies
the questioner, a woman
who in her past life never
lacked something to do,
always busy, always finding
another job to complete.
How hard it must be
when one's work is over
and there's nothing left to do.

Mantle of Invisibility

She didn't know exactly when it happened,
but one day she realized she had become invisible,
no longer seen by men or women or sometimes
even loved ones, whether she was alone
or in a crowd. She wondered what had changed,
why no one seemed to notice when she came
into a room or wore a new dress or a cool pair
of shoes. *When did this happen*, she wondered.
Was it when she let her gray hair show or when
she started wearing glasses or when she shed
the Spanxx? Was it when she allowed
the wrinkles to go uninjected and the puppet lines
to grow and grow? At first it hurt to know that
she had fallen and could not get up
from the dreaded pit of redundancy. In denial
she fought back, trying harder, scratching her way
into view albeit as fleeting as a glimpse.
When did this happen, she repeated to herself.

With time her viewpoint shifted and she gathered
the mantle around her, the new secret identity
pleasing her. To her surprise, the cloak fit well
and flattered with a new kind of comfort and strength.
She transformed into Invisible Woman and reset
her filters to block earworms like "*anti-aging*,"
"*granny arms*," and "*looking good for her age*."
Invisible Woman grew to enjoy her newfound power
to slip about unseen,
unmonitored,
unfettered,
unfazed,
and ultimately unashamed of her truth.
The cost of being seen was too high a price to pay.

July 9th, 2016

Last time we walked an aisle
together was our wedding day,
years ago, two children,
nine cars, seven houses,
countless pounds ago. This
time, our first-born escorts us
down gentle grassy steps
in soft end-of-day light
as music plays. We each
take a turn, embracing him,
then letting go.

Retreat, This Time Last Year

The path to Walker Percy's bench is strewn
with large elongated acorns, bright green
but yellow beneath the hull. I spotted
the same kind this time last year. Yesterday's
rain on the Cumberland Plateau brought them
to ground level, good fortune to each crow,
squirrel and red fox crossing these woods. In
the meadow two white-tails bolt for cover
when they hear or smell or see me. Are they
the same ones I saw this time last year? The
surroundings feel unchanged as if the place
awaited my return. Did winter come,
or spring and summer? I see no signs of
change. Sunrise casts the same long shadows.
Each step turns gravel, each view churns bits of
memory. I walk on, down the road to
the state park, the one with a natural
stone bridge. I pass a small, once-tended house
near the Church of God and remember it
from last fall, before the election, when
I'd wondered how many rooms and people
fit its tight floorplan. Maybe a tiny
living room, a kitchen, bedroom, perhaps
two. Close to the ditch I see the same bold
mailbox that had begged attention this time
last year, its side plastered with one man's full
name—Ralph Elster Thomas Jr.—in large
gold stick-on letters, the kind sold at the
hardware store. He must live alone, I think,
figuring such a large presence left scant
space inside for another living soul.

But there's something different, I decide,
seeing a huge sycamore tree is down
but untouched in the side yard. Dried brown
yucca stalks stand like spears guarding the
perimeter. The grass needs mowing and
the house needs painting. I have never laid
eyes on the man with the gold-lettered name,
but I worry he must be sick or hurt
or something tragic has befallen him.
Why has he let his house run down? A flash
of memory surges and I recall
this time last year a candidate's sign in
red, white and blue stood in his yard. The sign
is gone but its afterimage rockets me
back to present. Everything has changed.
Nothing feels the same. Nothing is the same.
This time last year I never imagined
that *grab her by the pussy* wouldn't matter.
Or that Russians tinkering behind the
curtains wouldn't matter. Who knew a swath
of chaos could be cut in such short order?
I never imagined the unhooded,
unashamed faces of hate carrying
torches through Charlottesville, hate that leads to
killing, hate that each day divides, conquers,
builds walls, pulls up ladders, closes doors to
so many others. This time last year I
never imagined how much our world could
change. Nothing feels the same. Nothing is the
same. Why have we let our house run down?

Suburban Spring

Whiffs hint of mulch, lawn
chemicals, lilacs from front-
vented laundry rooms.

Count the Stitches

The tiniest stitches hold it all together,
almost invisible to the casual eye.
Strong, tight thread tacks layers of fabric
and cotton in place, now pillowed
and puckered from daily use, repeated
washing, picnics on the grass, trips
to the beach. A design of utility
and art, its multi-colored fan-shaped
cloth pieces lives, loves, moments.
A red corduroy romper once worn by
an unsteady toddler. A first-day-of-school
plaid. A paper-thin white dotted Swiss
from sixth-grade graduation when
homemade dresses still satisfied the wearer.
The tiniest of stitches hold it all together,
almost invisible to those who feel its warmth.

Where Daffodils Remain

Each spring daffodils mark where home used to be.
The house is gone but her flowers still rise in March,
a reliable flash of yellow signaling winter's end,
awaiting hands to reach for them and place upon
the table. Vase and table now reside hundreds of miles
away, family pieces chipped and scratched but passed
like treasure to the next generation. Years ago the barn
collapsed into a pile of lumber and rusty tin but
the apple tree blooms in April to bear fruit in late
summer that rots on the ground. Such a waste, she would
have said, knowing that those same plantings had kept
her family fed, her table decorated. Hen house and garage
are down. White peonies and scarlet poppies bloom
in May, sweet peas climb in June, blackberries ripen
in July, lilies resurrect in August. Her buried treasures
collect strength, unseen, then reappear year after
year to bloom and bear with no one left to gather.

The Other Side

I am from the other side,
brought by those seeking
the gap where daylight
flowed between mountains.

I am from the other side,
brought east to west
on a lifelong journey
looking toward the sun.

I am from the other side,
a place in between,
both steep and flat, from
narrowest holler, widest sky.

I am from the other side,
hybrid native and alien,
neither *us* nor *them*.
I am from the other side.

Author's Acknowledgments

To my family, particularly Alex, Alexander, John and Allysan for their love, support and reading patience as I've made a midlife path correction back toward writing. The same goes for my sister Nancy, another first-line reader and cheerleader. A special thank you goes to Kentucky poet Savannah Sipple for reading and encouraging my venture into poetry.

And many thanks to the folks at the Appalachian Writers' Workshop, the Carnegie Center for Literacy and Learning, and Rivendell Writers Colony for inspiring writers to stretch and try new ways. It's never too late.

Jayne Moore Waldrop is a writer and attorney who served as literary arts liaison at the Carnegie Center for Literacy and Learning in Lexington, Kentucky. She is a graduate of the University of Kentucky (B.A., J.D.) and Murray State University's MFA in Creative Writing Program, and her work has appeared in the *Anthology of Appalachian Writers, Still: The Journal, New Madrid Journal, Appalachian Heritage, Minerva Rising, New Limestone Review, The Paddock Review, Sequestrum, Heartland Review, Luna Station Quarterly, Kudzu,* and *Deep South Magazine.* Her stories have been selected as Judge's Choice in the 2016 *Still Journal* Fiction Contest; finalists for the 2015 Reynolds Price Fiction Prize, the 2016 Tillie Olsen Fiction Award, and 2017 *Still Journal* Fiction Contest; and honorable mention in the 2014 AWP Intro Journals Project. Her poetry chapbook *Retracing My Steps* was a finalist in the 2018 New Women's Voices Chapbook Competition. A former book columnist for the Louisville *Courier-Journal,* she served two terms on the Kentucky Arts Council and is a Kentucky Foundation for Women grant recipient. Her family includes husband Alex; sons Alexander and John; daughter-in-law Allysan; Cuddles and Daisy Finch.

CPSIA information can be obtained
at www.ICGtesting.com
Printed in the USA
BVHW071100130819
555662BV00016B/2536/P